synchronicity

Collected Poems

by
Thomas Zampino

synchronicity

Collected Poems

by Thomas Zampino

synchronicity

By Thomas Zampino

First Edition

Author: Thomas Zampino
Editor: Paul Gilliland
Formatting: Southern Arizona Press
All Artwork: Pixabay.com

Published by Southern Arizona Press
Sierra Vista, Arizona 85635
www.SouthernArizonaPress.com

ISBN: 978-1-960038-02-9

Poetry

"If you're tuned in, life feels like a story" - David Sedaris

And when you're really tuned in, every story reads likes poetry.

Moments of synchronicity - seemingly unconnected acts of "co-incidences" - help make us better observers and storytellers.

Something here, something there happening simultaneously may or may not be connected - or perhaps not connected in ways that we can understand.

But through observation, through imagination, through a conscious stepping back, we can patch together a single, coherent, interconnected story.

And poetry is the glue that holds it all together.

Listen, observe, be open to all the sounds and movements around you. Enter into those moments without fear. Tell about them without regret.

And know that every story written today is really just tomorrow's poetry.

Dedication

To those with stories left to tell - and the poets within them.

Each of these poems / poetic observations have appeared at https://thomaszampino.wordpress.com/ and a handful have previously appeared in *Precise Moment* by Thomas Zampino.

Contents

synchronicity

four decades in and the story first appeared

the prologue promised love

    and hope

       and dreams

the middle proved that detours

    are just new beginnings

the final chapters insisted

    that we look both forward and back

four decades in and it occurs to me

that our steps were never linear

    because as we crossed over

       from circle to circle together

we simply kept expanding our world along the way

A Single Kiss

There was a time that I didn't see you.

There was a time I dared not know.

But today you opened my eyes

    and brushed away the tears

        from sweet memories that

            have so often failed me.

A single kiss can

    sometimes be

        just like that.

Just One Word

Sometimes, it's just one word.

Sometimes, it's just one kiss.

Sometimes, it's the silence.

Each holds the power

Each turns the key

   that can change

      everything –

Just as you

   did me.

A Moment Of Alchemy

A moment of alchemy slipped in between us

as we circled in rhythm for the first time

even with awkward feet still learning.

A turn,

a smile,

a waltz,

a blur.

The room behind us disappearing.

Two of us,

transported somewhere outside.

But then landing safely.

Just in time.

Looking Back

It was inconceivable,

    but never truly impossible.

It was a far-off journey

    but resided in our own backyard.

It was an eternity away

    but began anew just a moment ago.

It overturned everything

    but all things have remained unchanged.

It was a commitment made thirty years ago,

    but really only yesterday.

Thomas Zampino

Through Thirty-Five Years

Through thirty-five years
  it's become increasingly obvious
    that we were not two halves
      desperate to become as one,
    but rather two complete mortal beings
  who joined together, freely in love,
only to find along the way
  that we've made each other
    stronger,
      wiser,
        more loving,
          more miraculous
  than we ever could have imagined on our own.
Two instruments completely transformed
  through one extraordinary symphony.

You Have Always Known That

Passion can overturn the status quo
    while affirming the truth that binds it.
Passion can engage the folly of men
    while bidding them to seek peace.
But rare is the one who sees the truth
    who knows from whence it comes.
Passion is a song at home in the soul
    and a heart that cleaves to the wind.
You have always known that.

What Matters

I came to you bearing my heart,
    my soul,
        my entire life.
I was never certain of acceptance or rejection
    but that never once mattered.

We built a home,
    a family,
        an entire life.
I was never certain of permanence
    but that never once mattered.

The kids have left,
    we've started over.
I was never certain of the days left
    and that has always mattered.

Enough

Side by side and hand in hand,
    neither of us sure about what comes next.
Two score years of exhaustive honesty,
    backhanded compliments, and salt –
        that sometimes flavor enhancer
        equally adept at intensifying old wounds.

Nothing about the walk still ahead
    will permit even a hint of pretense or pride.
Nothing about it will charm us into believing
    that we can start back over again.
Only the two of us,
    side by side
        and hand in hand,
            willing to just be.

And today,
            that's enough.

What Remains Behind

The sticky sweet smell of a sleeping newborn,

the liquidating heat dancing between lovers,

and the worn-down obsessions of youth.

Memories rarely ever get these right

but who would ever trade them?

Ordinary Moments

Memories came flooding back today.

Simple things,

    like when I grabbed your hand

        for the very first time

    and when you touched my heart

        for the very last.

Two ordinary moments

    that forever mixed up everything.

That set everything on fire

    before we ever learned about forgetting.

Ordinary moments are sometimes like that,

    even if memories are not.

Overlapping Circles

We are

    Overlapping circles.

A part of me undeniably you

    Concentric circles

Anchored toward one center

    Tangent circles

Connected,

    never consumed.

And So Here I Am

We can cherish without loving
　　but even allies will betray.
　　　　We are not yet one.

We can fall back into hardness
　　but even stones are made to bleed.
　　　　We are not yet stone.

We can drink from midnight's madness
　　but even darkness takes its leave.
　　　　We are not yet night.

And so here I am.

Creating Silence, Creating Freedom

Deep breath in, deep breath out.

A moment of silence in between.

Capture that space.

Extend it up.

Bring it back down.

Freedom and release.

Seconds exchanged for

a time incalculable but complete

1 . . .

    2 . . .

       3 . . .

          4 . . .

            5 . . .

              6

Free

Last night's cry for help was the loudest yet,
    wrapped as it was in stone-cold silence.
I am no longer shocked by your pain,
    but neither am I frightened by it.

Miles apart, there are simultaneous forces at work,
    ones greater than either of us will ever understand.
It is in the letting go of make believe,
    of dreams, of desperate midnight pleas,
    that you can be free.

Now at your weakest,
    now at rest within that otherwise imperceptible space
    between reality and illusion,
    you can finally bargain for your strength.

Underground Play

I see you most mornings on the subway
    seated in that very same place.
You take up more than your share of space.
Brawny, bearded, some might even call you a badass
    with that gold earring and thick chain hanging low.
But we all know your little secret,
    we see it.
The look on your face,
    the gestures,
        give it away.

synchronicity

Yesterday,

    you bent your head down

    so that the little boy

    you carried in that stroller

    could reach up to play

    with your hat.

And then he smiled at you

    with that one tooth smile.

And you returned it.

Then you saw me watching you both,

    right before you got off,

    just as we both nodded.

Knowingly.

(Previously Published in The University of Chicago's *Memoryhouse*
    Magazine)

In the Letting Go

Surrendering first to the colors of aging
    and soon enough delivered by the wind,
    there is no more graceful exit
    than a leaf letting go in the fall.

For all its insignificance there seems much,
    still, to take away.
But I am neither moved nor envious.
For I am not a leaf
And not at all graceful in the letting go.

A Bell, A Life

I heard it again yesterday.

A bell ringing in who knows what.

A call to service?

In memory of a life?

Clarity to vibrato to short-lived stillness.

Hashed and rehashed without competition.

Only to be overtaken by the sounds of the night

    with just a stone-cold silence

    left ringing in my head.

Surrender

A memory flashes from years before.
Or was it only a dream?
I can no longer really tell the difference
    between things once coveted
    and those lost along the way.
Nothing much remains
    except the exhilarating smell of youth,
    and even that is fading.

Memories may well anchor my present,
    but they have also buried my past.
And tomorrow remains just some illusion,
    well hidden behind walls that are still being built.

I was once told about a line resting somewhere
    between self-deception and reality.
I've long since learned that it's moving target,
    one easily breached.
Memories and dreams are very much like that.
Once we discover how to surrender them both.

Stones

Impenetrable as they sometimes are,
    stones exude a surprising softness.
A heart of stone still beats with fleshy imprecision
    and earthly attachment.
An old stone fence still tenders its fullest protections
    against the winds.
And boys skipping stones often find themselves
    also casting memories.
Impenetrable as they sometimes are,
    stones can be surprisingly yielding.

Concentric Circles

One inside the other

    neither touching nor ignoring.

Shapes defined by outer strength

    and inner vulnerability.

Yielding for a moment

    to infinite possibility –

            conceding nothing

Light

Light can tempt the dark spaces hiding between us
    without demanding allegiance or acknowledgment.
Light can appeal to kinship in our times of loneliness
    without binding itself to our distractions and failures.
Light can easily be severed or thought unsustainable
    without anguishing over the inevitableness of its loss.

Whispers Through the Night

The in and out of her breathing opens the space

    between tonight's restlessness

    and tomorrow's forgetfulness,

    guiding me throughout the night

    like some ancient but impossible song.

Then a whisper, a sigh,

    an unconscious movement

    unleashes memories not yet lived

    but were always meant to be.

Eloquence

Words alone are never more eloquent than silence
    nor the body more powerful than a wounded soul.
If you are fully awake, you are fully alone
    but not in a way that can measure loss
    for beauty still resides alongside you
    and truth somewhere in between
    all of the silent spaces.

Already

Sitting just across from me,

    you looked away pretending the whole time.

    But I already knew who you were.

Walking towards our life together,

    you focused straight ahead.

    But I already knew we could never turn back.

Raising our babies amid chaos and fun,

    your face spoke of exhaustion.

    But I already knew every surrender only brought us

        closer.

Holding your hand as you slipped away,

    the night wrapped around us one last time.

    But I already knew I would find you again.

No doubt sitting just across from me.

No longer just pretending.

All These Things are Broken

All these things are broken
    and I was once the man to fix them,
but I'm older now,
                and tired too,
and there will always be more to fix,
so, I'll let them be,
                just like me.

                    (broken has its place)

Traveling Back In Time a Bit

Traveling back in time a bit,
    heading off to school in the middle of a storm
I well remember the sharp scent
    of the lightening as it split the morning,
terrifying my companions
    as I pretended some uncommon courage.
Memories should always allow for some forbearance,
    I think,
A forgiveness on the part of the holder
    to make our destined lives
    fit so much neater into the crafted narrative
    that moves us to the next day.
But I best not jot any of that down
    so I can (without deceit) look back tomorrow
    and pretend some uncommon wisdom.

Dirt

We walk atop it
   ignoring its weight
   until smothered …
      Dirt.

But a seed first buried
   has yet to die,
   sucking life like a babe in arms …
      Dirt.

We push back, mostly
   then gather in anger
   misunderstanding …
      Dirt.

Thomas Zampino

In the Rain

Walking together in the rain,

    we stopped for a moment under a tree.

Each leaf already a tiny cymbal,

    each drop firing off a different beat.

I remember how bright your face glistened

    every time the sky lit up.

But that glow lasted long after we started back

    on our way,

lighting our path, easing my mind,

    knowing that the rains had arrived again

Just in time

        Just like they always do

Curiosities

What makes the sky blue, the grass green,
    the sun appear yellow?
What causes the soul to leap, music to heal,
    a touch to be miraculous?

If ego alone ruled the heart,
    we'd miss every opportunity
    to see ourselves embedded in every color,
    every connection,
    every act of reckless abandon.

We are as fortunate in our sorrows
    as we are in our expectations,
    both leading us to wander off
    in unforeseen directions,
    capturing the fullness
    of today's curiosities.

And always, in the end,
    leaving us to grasp
    at life's most exquisite conclusions.

Thomas Zampino

Preconceptions

A single moment shaped everything:

The color of your skin,

the food on your table,

your survival beyond some foolish childhood dreams

mixed in from generations unknown,

unaware,

unforeseen.

Before your parents were acknowledged,

you were unleashed

Atom by atom,

cell by cell,

thought by thought,

ratified through love.

While nothing was set in stone,

nothing really changes.

Affix Yourself

Affix yourself to the day
    as you would to each other.
Your days remaining aren't everything
    but they're not unimportant.

Affix yourself to the night
    as does the moon to the sky.
Your dreams aren't everything
    but they often help point the way.

Affix yourself to your soul
    as the oceans have to the earth.
Your steps aren't everything
    but nothing long abides unnoticed.

Mixtures

If I could mix the pale blue sky

    with the sounds of your laughter,

        I would never find my way home again.

If I could mix this sweet rose

    with the touch of your hand,

        I would somehow find time for just one more day.

If I could mix my existence

    with the soft rhythms of your breath,

        I would forever confess to having lived a miracle.

Rumblings in the Night

A sigh followed by a whisper,
    a whisper yielding to a curse.
Warning signs abound for those still looking,
    even more so for those refusing to try.
Sleep has become a distraction,
    while time just reveals its lies
awakening me again to the rumblings …
    the rumblings in the night.

Momentary Lull

The clock on the mantle stopped last night,

    sometime around midnight.

As if unsure of itself,

    or contemplating whether one more sweep around

    was even necessary.

I really shouldn't read too much

    into the actions of a generations-old time piece

    that has been keeping an eye on us

    these past twenty years, now at rest.

But its momentary lull reminds me

    that there is something,

perhaps in the stepping back,

    that can strip darkness of its power

    and corruption of its grip.

Once surrender no longer measures loss.

Seedlings

If you cannot even imagine anything

    beyond the sanctuary and the safety

    with which you have already comforted yourself,

why would you ever risk planting a seed?

Thomas Zampino

Philosophical Leaves

A tree in the garden,

    even one hellbent on disguising its purpose,

can't help but reveal its fruit

    to every soul that walks by.

Even its leaves tell the story,

    first of fits and starts,

then of a falling away,

    season upon season.

How very much like the rest of us.

Just Before I Go

Sometimes,
    the world's anger swallows us up.
More often
    it seems the other way around.
But it's the troubled heart
    that still moves mountains,
and a doleful hand
    that stirs the seas.
So, here I stand,
    ready now to learn from you . . .
Just before I go.

Reaching Back

From this angle,

      sitting on my front porch,

   the branches and the leaves

   on that lusty tree across the way

   appear to be propping up the sun.

Holding it in place for just a few more moments,

   before it finally slips away beyond the night.

A brief, humble ceremony

   given over to acknowledge a simple daily debt.

Just before the letting go.

It left me wondering

   whether memories are truly ever kind.

   They remind us too easily of those days

   soaked in drink and ease and youthful vigor.

Only to suddenly slam us with the knowledge that we,

   too, traded them all in for a handful of lies,

   never looking back.

   And that we would likely do it all again

   if given the chance.

synchronicity

But maybe we were meant to have something more

in common with those branches

and those leaves across the way.

Holding on to a single day.

A day without any before it.

Just before the letting go.

Of Hearts That Bleed

The heart itself is a double mixed bag.
    Forever
Desperate for acknowledgement and safety and solace,
    yet presuming that blood need never be spilled.
But there can be no warmth, no surety,
    no abiding open space
without first some grand strutting through every jeopardy,
    every wager, every humbling death.

Something Less Than Silence

Even the quiet that we hear
  when there is no sound
speaks louder than the silence
  offered up by the earth
when it finally
  welcomes us back home.

Down Time

The hardest part of loneliness is not the silence,

    nor the feeling of isolation.

It's not the boredom

    that comes from mindless anticipations

    and wondering when they'll end

and while the slowing down of the days,

    the hours,

      and the minutes is still mostly difficult

the hardest part of loneliness,

    in the end,

      is in the being alone …

                next to someone else.

There Is No Time Left for Living

The days are softening,
   but the nights remain incomplete.
Blurred lines, mixed up memories,
   long abandoned detours lie ahead.
If yesterday never happened,
   tomorrow becomes just so much collateral damage
and once every breath needs to last a lifetime,
   there is no time left for living.
Sometimes mutiny best serves the unnerved heart.

The House of Music

There's a front room that you can walk through,
    if you just want to catch a note or two.
But the back door is always open
    and you can settle right in.
Some nights, the music will lift you up.
    Others will just bring you down.
Either way,
    you'll want to stay all night.
Because here, you'll be ripped to pieces,
    then put right back together again.
But never in the same way
    and always with a chance to start over.
Isn't that what you've always wanted,
    like you once told me?
Everything out there will be forgotten.
What happens in here insists on forever,
    until it's over.
In this place, that we call the house of music.
    come dance.

Window Shadows

Window shadows
They misshape,
   misrepresent,
      and mostly miss the mark.
Yet, they remind us,
   that our reality often bends
      back towards some unmet need
and that what is real may no longer exist,
   what exists may no longer be real,
knowing all the while,
   that when I reach out,
      that shadow will splinter off
and land right back on me,
   if only for a moment.

A Very Modest Proposal

At the beginning of the day and not at the end
 should be the time for acceptance and reality.
The time that we are the most vulnerable and
 the most receptive.
We can change the world or really just ourselves
 while believing we are changing the world.
And at the end of the day,
 that's probably just enough to make it happen.

Our Future's Past

Taking your hands for the first time

    reminded me of our future.

The kids we raised, the home we furnished,

    the trace of death already passed but not yet begun.

A kiss sealed the memories

    that have tried to wake us in our old age

unsuccessfully at first

    but now delightfully ruinous.

That seems to be the trouble with the future,

    always looking for a comfortable past to hide in.

Red

Red is both the color of anger

and a reminder of love.

It points to death in the fall

and the force in our veins.

Red sounds an alarm

yet commands us to stop.

It reflects deep in the sea

and back to the sky.

Red is our invitation to life.

Royal's Blue

There are too many reasons to remember
    why blue calls to me the way that it does.
Perhaps it's the sky's moving canvas
    or the ocean's nomadic mirrors
that long ago fooled me
    into seeing it everywhere.
Yet it's the rare sight of robin's eggs,
    sapphire eyes,
        and lapis lazuli artistry
            that first drew royalty to its charms.
As for me,
            I'll just gently cling to its indelible beauty.

Thomas Zampino

Timely

The shorter days
    make it abundantly clear to me,
        if it wasn't already,
that a clock is designed neither to record
    a lifetime of movement
        nor its direction.

Its only job is to stand between us
    and the seconds it counts off
        while reminding observers
that the way ahead requires nothing more
    than an acknowledgment of the past
        while not being held hostage to it.

Reflections Through Shattered Glass

Looking back,

        looking up,

                looking in.

A moment can last forever,

    eternity but an instant.

Our beliefs often hinge

    upon what it is we are looking for.

Our reality,

    our authenticity,

        eventually settle upon what we find.

But there's no danger in the questioning,

    and no peril in the pursuit.

Except in the failure to try.

Torn Places

The clumsiness,
   the false starts,
the perpetual hijacking
   leave the torn places
     raw and abraded.
But that's where most stories begin

One Embrace

I set my arms around you.

    My hands intertwined behind your back.

You are always free to go.

    My touch bound only through your love.

This is how I envision it.

    The keen embrace of heaven and earth.

Belief

I've always been a believer.

The shadows may have changed

    but the flame never stopped dancing.

A recognition that the ground beneath us

    is teeming with life

        and the seed of our own.

An understanding

    that mathematical equations

        alone cannot measure the power

            within a first breath

and giving me the time

    and opportunity to binge on life

even when nothing else

    seems to fit quite right anymore.

Now

I rise, I stumble, I get up again.

Every day seemed just like every other.

Every path I had chosen led me back here

. . . except now . . .

Now there is learning, there is growth, there is love

and, quite miraculously, now there is you.

I still rise, stumble, and get up again.

But each day is different

because we walk

together

now.

And We are Now One, Forever

Shades of darkness,

    degrees of time.

Morning sun how sweet,

    sublime.

Cool winds split the night from day.

Then we rise and walk away

    and we are now one,

        forever.

Give

To give in

    often robs us of our existence.

To give up

    revokes our promises to others.

To give away

    is to gather up all eternity.

Even

Even the bravest among us
    cannot outpace death,
        we can only abide.

Even the fiercest among us
    cannot use force in search of love,
        we will only be defeated.

Even the hate within us
    cannot survive without the love of another,
        we are never truly free.

Ancient Promises

Walk with me back to the earth
  and let your lungs fill with ancient promises.
Hidden just below the surface
  are the eternal roles for which we first auditioned.
Ever mindful of our place,
  we know that what has come before
    will never be again,
and what has yet to be
  was never promised.
Yet we remain curious creatures,
  much like the gods in those locked away stories.
Our jealousies and weaknesses
  fuel our desires as often as they rouse our enemies.
We know the story well.
There is always one more bargain,
  always one more attempt to derail the inevitable.
Yet the very things that can move us beyond hope
  remain untouched, unrecognized.
It's time to unearth those ancient promises.

Thomas Zampino

Witness to Myself

Sometimes I step aside
    to let my younger self pass.
The body receives its fate with equal parts
    equanimity and stubbornness.
While the mind still repels every advance
    that doesn't offer some way out.
And here I stand,
    a witness to myself laughing at both.

Move On

Slowly,

    deliberately,

        mindfully,

            enthusiastically.

There's a gate through which you will pass today

    whether you are ready to enter it,

        whether you are not.

And it closes suddenly,

    without warning,

        all at once.

You can't go back.

    But why would you want to?

You no longer exist there.

    No one ever does.

So, move on my child.

    Move on.

Dare to Go First

Don't enter the evening without having noticed that smile,
    that touch,
        that laugh,
            that gentle voice,
                that childlike grace.
Each of these abound
    as surely as do their gloomy and dismal rivals.
We need only look for them
    upon the return of our own.
Dare to go first.

The World is Waiting

The world is waiting for your touch.
    Will you deny it?
There is a holy presence within you
    no one else has.
Indelibly engraved with your unique
    course and code.
You are its sole keeper, its guardian,
    awaiting dispatch.
It's why you are here in this moment
    and were selected.

Who We Are

We are divisible,

    we are fundamentally one.

Warriors and peacemakers,

    tinkerers and artists,

        builders and destroyers.

Double minded pursuers

    with single minded dreams.

Together we fuse the night's burdens

    with tomorrow's promises.

Look upward,

    look ahead.

We are divisible,

    we are fundamentally one.

First Breath, Last Breath
(A Father's Cry)

It's not my story to tell,
  not my tears that have fallen.
But who can listen
  without completely breaking?

In the birthing room to cut the cord,
    to hold the child,
        to dance with the first breath.
In the ER to re-suture the wounds,
    to hold the child,
        to rage against the last breath.

Rebuking the healers,
    despising the hour.
Coming full circle,
    an ending without closure.

Spring

The sweet smell of spring
    brushes up against my nose.
Inhale, exhale as if for the first time,
    and maybe the last.
I'm not concerned either way.
    Not my place to question.
A moment to stand still –
    leaning forward   (looking back)
Always the same direction,
    always in the same moment
until tomorrow brings me twenty steps closer,
    or farther.

Set Aside

Set aside yesterday's broken promises.

Set aside today's unhealed heart.

Extraordinary gifts are rarely revealed

    in extraordinary moments

– even the rain understands.

August

Sundown comes earlier now.
Racing against the clock
    and setting up the nighttime sky.
The cool breezes of autumn
    slowly introduce themselves
as if somehow unknown to us
but the ground remembers,
    even if the leaves have no way
of knowing what happens next.
I am not a leaf.

Colors

Vibrant and vulnerable,
    restless and reflective.
The leaves absorb the autumn light,
    then spit it out.
Returning the reds, browns, and yellows
    that wink at death
While going about their work
    in quiet seriousness without delay.

Summer Mist

The marsh still holds back
    a secret or two from this inhibited city dweller.
The silence can be as unnerving as it is inviting.
Rarely for me does an ordinary day
    pass uninterrupted by sirens,
the hot urgencies of some trembling subway tracks,
    and street music
both unadorned and unrequited.
It's a rhythm one soon enough adopts as their own.

But today, solitary, unfiltered quiet.
My body is bathed in the steamy, rolling mist
    that quickly disappears just behind me.
And the liquid smell
    reminds me just how far I've traveled.
Not a trace of freshly poured concrete
    or stale city sweat
        remains on my clothes
            or in my brain.
There's not enough time here to breathe it all in.

But my lungs and my blood
    will carry a part of this all back with me.
And then, when I can finally open my eyes again,
    I'll remember the quiet.

Mysteries and Trust

They really aren't mysteries anymore.
Those things that sometimes kept us awake at nights
    wondering,
        compelling us toward higher ground
            by casting us down to our knees.
Too numerous to count,
    some musings appeared far too uncertain
        to be trustworthy
            or even minimally acceptable.
Yet there they were.

And they were just as real to us,
    just as practical,
        just as inviting
            as the local coffee shop.
Their existence seemed always to point
    toward a way out,
        convincing us of our rectitude.

But drowning in information,

    we are now too afraid to breathe.

When every question can be unlocked by a fingerprint,

    imagination finds itself hiding

        somewhere beyond the next offering of fact.

Speculation long ago became an anomaly

    and doubt itself is enough to be feared.

Yet we probably still sense

    that not every answer is necessary,

        not every data set worthwhile,

            not every mystery need be quickly solved.

If only we can remember how to trust.

Brilliant Reminder

Soft autumn winds cannot long stand
    against the hard push rushing in from behind.
The cold, damp air prevails
    but not without some surprise
        at its sudden dominance.
Soon itself to fall victim to the sky's seeming fickleness –
    one obsessively planned,
A brilliant reminder of our own capriciousness
    as we rail against the bonds of false security.

At Last

At last,

    the leaves are beginning to turn.

At last,

    the damp ground is turning solid.

Summer bids goodbye with no regrets

    and fall takes its place quietly (for now).

I am ready.

    I am ready for the cold.

I am ready.

    I am ready for the dark.

I am ready at last for the patience

    that I can no longer abandon.

White Rabbit

It's hard to see him,

    the white rabbit

        matched up against the snow.

Only his dark and brooding eyes

    pop from the powdery drifts.

Is he cold?

    Scared?

        Hungry?

Or just some angel-like creature

    sent to watch over me?

To see how I'd react.

    To test my character and resolve.

Is he warmth?

    Confidence?

        Food?

synchronicity

I invest too much
    in the things that cross my path
Or, perhaps, not enough sometimes.
    Like now.

It's hard to know him,
    the white rabbit
        matched up against the snow.

December

December races towards the new year
    with abandon.
The short days
    making short work of our plans
Gifts (anxiety),
    parties (anxiety),
        time's up! (relief)

Checking boxes,
    filling boxes,
        feeling boxed in.
Then, in rapid slow motion,
    frigid nights hawk warm embraces
and yet another chance to start over
    in the clear, blue, cold.

Melancholy Markers

Dancing leaves in the silky night air.

I often thought I could find you there.

Silvery nights and darkening days.

A wink at time that has slipped away.

Tomorrow brings its own embrace

of reminders that I cannot erase.

The soft volition of your body.

The sweet alliance with your soul.

Shadow Dance

A neighbor's roof
    provides a temporary canvas
upon which winter limbs
    dance through shadows
Branches soon re-fleshed
    by the warm spring sun
arouse ancient veins
    to nourish their latest charges.

Reposition

Overnight the familiar aroma of renewal
    began its slow, downward descent.
First hints of airborne irritants, real or imagined,
    settle in my throat
as the full weight of my body
    lets the ground give way, ever so slightly.
Leaves, dirt, and the squirming life
    just below the surface
prepare to reposition themselves
    away from the hibernation, isolation,
and deathless quiet
    of a winter still negotiating its surrender.

Leaves

Drinking in the wet summer,

    the trees around my house are thriving.

Spring may now have come to a full stop,

    but preparation for what lies ahead continues.

Each robust breath in

    concedes to a more labored breath out.

And today's peak greens

    will soon abandon themselves

to tomorrow's reds, and yellows,

    and the irresistible coming breach.

But fall will always remain my favorite.

Time enough to savor

    the beauty of the day,

and wisdom enough to appreciate

    the comfort of the night.

And even stripped of all cover,

    I can still find winter's harsh indifference

        to be more amusing than frightening.

Much like the trees around my house.

So today, I'll just enjoy the endless rain.

But I'm still going to keep an eye on those trees.

Ah, the Fall

Beautiful,
    softly colored leaves
        gently floating downward through the air,
cool days
    followed by cuddly,
        warm blanketed nights,
and the sound of acorns and pine cones
    incessantly smashing into every car,
        street,
            and living soul
                as if the trees themselves
were starting their advance on enemy territory.

Age

Age gives us certain permission
    to see those things
we had always assumed
    were better left unnoticed.
Whether the shallowness of friendship
    or the vanity of our self-centered belief
in our abilities to get past the humiliations
    and indiscretions of a broken world.

We had thought ourselves better than that.
    But with permission comes understanding
and a chance to engage common ground,
    to walk back our incessant fears,
finding ourselves entangled
    with connectedness and detachment
in some full and equal measures
    shedding our impenetrable crust.

Thomas Zampino

Rhythm

Asking the sun to rise an hour earlier
    or the moon to pierce the night sky
        changes nothing.

Asking the tide to hold back its promises
    so that we can navigate the sea
        changes nothing.

Asking ourselves to feel today's rhythm
    with patience and understanding
        changes us.

And that just might change everything.

Dashes and Blank Spaces

Dates set in stone,

one of which is known

Remains a blank space,

soon enough to be erased

Breathing in through the dash,

we indulge every vicious contrast

And so, surrender too early our souls

Horizon

The mouth of the horizon,
    even with pursed lips,
        joins heaven and earth.
We can only envy that border
    as we cross the landscape
        or sail the seas.
For there is no path for us to reach it,
    no mechanism with which to touch
        its volcanic stillness
 – one that erupts in stone-age silence
    only to retreat in soft repose.
We are, at long last,
    so much the same.

We are as One at Night

We are as one at night

    for sleep upends even our cruelest disentanglements.

Our dreams are connected,

    our breath drawn from the same midnight air.

And so, there is no chance

    to avoid the pain and sorrow all around

until we awaken once more

    to the morning's light.

Fine Lines

There's a fine line
    between genius and disaster
and if you extend that line outward
    and forever
it's altogether possible
    that line curves up
before it cycles back down,
    then crisscrossing
ten or forty
    or one thousand twenty-four more times
between epic failure,
    and some outsized magic-laced result
without ever knowing which one was true
    or whether it ever really mattered.

Speak to Me of Luminous Things

Speak to me of luminous things,
    things that get me through the night.
Of shiny swords and cold bright faces
    that walk us back to safety.

Speak to me of everlasting things,
    things that reveal their undying presence.
Of coldhearted stones and fortified castles
    that one day will outlive us.

Speak to me of mundane things,
    things that ease my mind and split the day.
Of overdue bills and long forgotten memories
    that never really understand.

Measures

At first, they seem to intertwine,
　　deep in the middle of the night.
Measured beats,
　　taking turns,
as if some percussionist were racing between
　　my alarm clock and the bathroom sink.

A sharp-tongued steady tick
　　followed by an inexhaustible delicate flop.
Then a return trip.
　　And another after that.
Keeping score, keeping time.
　　Even as I try to sleep.

But the occasional off-beat can also be heard
　　if I pay long enough attention.
The faucet suddenly relieves itself
　　in a short, winding sigh.
One that makes the sink gurgle with delight,
　　eager as it is to consume the excess flow.

And then a quick return back to rhythm.

    Maybe not quite the same as before.

A new song,

    a different beat.

Sometimes the sounds are so completely in sync

    that just a single one thereafter splits the night.

At least for a time. At least until

    they can find a safe place to cycle back out again.

A reminder,

    here in these sleepless hours,

that time doesn't so much demand our constancy

    as it does our movement.

And, perhaps, just a bit of patience through it all.

Thomas Zampino

Sacred Ground

Looking out through my backyard window
    this early summer morning
– sitting at my kitchen table,
    sipping some warmed-over Starbucks coffee
        from my favorite Boston souvenir travel mug
– I unexpectedly began to understand something
    about my place here.

Like the space separating the trees
    that were seeded long before I was born
and the saplings that were planted just last week,
    I am permanently wedged between generations.

I've never been one to overestimate
    the importance of my brief time here.
There'll surely be no lasting consequence
    to anything I will ever personally accomplish
        no matter how well played.
And nothing that I will ever fail to do
    will exactly influence the historical record either.

But it's as a connector,
    a bridge between the old and the new,
        where some lasting value fully reveals itself.
That space,
    the fertile ground we occupy between generations,
can easily sustain growth
    while generating new, indestructible wisdom
– but only if we can first learn to absorb
    and synthesize whatever has come before us.

It's not necessary that we understand all of it,
    or even that we derive any personal value from it.
Our role is in the timing
    – knowing when to pass it on.
Otherwise, the space we occupy
    is little more than some back burned ground
where perplexed bystanders are content simply
    to stand around, ready only to snuff out
        every wildfire heading our way.
But not every fire need be extinguished.

I believe there is much sacred ground
    between generations.
And it's our job to stand firmly
    within that space as
        we hand off humanity's continually
unfolding testimony
    from one occupier to the next.

Surrender

You are never obligated to surrender to your anger, your
sadness,
    or even some antiquated presumption
        of unworthiness.
But recognize these self-concerned disruptions
    for what they really are:
A mangled and broken space
    through which you sometimes must crawl,
a narrow opening
    that can allow you to envision some better self,
and the ultimate proving ground
    of humanity's common blood flowing through you,
        that vulnerable life force connecting us one
            to the other.
Feelings pass.
    Emotions sometimes fail us.
Intensity dissipates.
    But you remain.
Even when you feel most compelled to surrender.

Just a Little More

Carry on, they say.

As if nothing at all matters.

As if all that happened began with one anxious dream.

But sometimes the ground beneath us

    trembles far too much.

When every step guarantees a fall.

It's difficult to brace your legs

    while your mind is untethered,

        unsteady,

           unsure.

Just a little more, they say.

A little more time, a little more effort.

And surely, just a little more focus on others.

It's solid, practical, reasonable advice of course.

And if I could absorb it,

    learn from it,

        embrace it,

           you know that I would.

synchronicity

As Jacob once wrestled, so too must I.

And I will also find a way,

    even though I limp.

Perhaps especially so.

But first today,

    let me sleep.

        Just a little more

The Old House

The old house is still standing,
    the one from my childhood.
It's much smaller than I remembered.
Maybe because my eyes –
    and my belly –
        are so much bigger now.
Too big for this old cape cod
built for lazy summer days
but later pressed into service
for a year-round family.
My favorite lookout spot, the dormers,
    are still firmly in place.

As I stand here, everything more easily comes into view:
The uneven floors,
    the unfinished bedrooms,
        the mismatched doorknobs,
            and broken countertops.
The youthful energy that once bounced off
    of nearly every darkened corner of this place.

And every dream I ever dreamed was born here.

Some many years ago forgotten.

Some, by the grace of God,

    were buried here,

in the backyard,

    along with the usual 1960's assortment of small,

        lovable, non-cuddly creatures.

But what I better understand,

    looking back,

is that it's still altogether possible

    to cram infinite amounts of love

and enchantment and wonder

    into an unforgivably finite space.

Even one that has always refused to hide

    its obsolescence and its poverty.

Thomas Zampino

Mirror

That those around us are sometimes cruel
    is not surprising.
Maybe it should be,
    but it's not.
There are times when we expect the worst from others,
    and times when we have no expectations at all.
Rarely are we disappointed.
But it's not as if kindness and generosity
    ever appear spontaneously,
        on their own and without cost.
We know better, because, well,
    just because we do.
And part of what we know
    is that every act of humanity,
        at its heart,
            at its beginning,
                is grounded in fraud.
Not necessarily a lie, mind you,
    but a fraud,
        a deception nonetheless.

116

Sometimes the protagonist,

    sometimes a bit player,

we offer the world a mirror

    when it's searching for a window.

I am you,

    you are me,

        and we pretend to dance to the same rhythm.

We hide until we are exposed.

    Until that mirror flips back around.

But that exposure,

    at long last,

        serves only to confirm our very worst fear –

        that we are, indeed,

            one and the same.

No, your selfishness,

    your hostility,

        even your cruelty

        can never take me by surprise.

Because, when I stand before you,

    I know full well who I really am.

River Flow

A river's instinct is to seek relief through movement,
    a framework that often ends in some final,
      perhaps noble,
        act of understated self-emptying.
In ways that only superficially matter,
    our lives seemingly have much in common
      with this quest for constant diversion.

Sometimes, momentary relief
    can be found through harmless
      psychological or physical distractions.
But too many of us become fixated
    on the ugliest forms of human behavior –
      whether our own or those of others.
And our simmering contempt
    quickly turns abusive
      if not outright self-destructive.

We may indeed find movement,
  but unlike that inexorable river flow,
    ours is almost always towards
      the things that are smaller,
        subordinate,
          more divisive.

In the end, we mostly turn inward.
Back towards the governing self.
But it needn't always end that way.

Destination and Choice

Destination is not only a matter of time,
    but of choice.
A direction chosen sets in motion
    forces both hidden and revealed.
By tapping into them,
    we can often learn how to separate ourselves
        from the momentary crisis –
            even if only long enough to regain a foothold.
Neither exigencies
    nor ordinariness need define us.
We remain free to engage with every moment
    on our own terms,
        guided by our own witness.
Whether we ever dare acknowledge it,
    every movement forward or back
        is a lesson taught to generations yet to come.
And so, we serve as either a signal of danger,
    or as a guide helping others to clear the brush.
Destination is not only a matter of time,
    but of choice.

Fences

Staring out the window of my back porch.
I'd guess the washed-out wooden fence
    separating neighbor from neighbor
        would be easier to breach
            than its metal-framed gate.
The one with the concrete stumps
    and rusted, broken latches.
What if only the gate were left standing?
A defined place from which to enter,
    when even the physical barriers between us
        no longer really mattered.
An explicit demarcation of personality
    and self-interest.
I think that's how you can best reach me.
Even if I tear down the fence,
    I'll keep the gate in good repair,
and you can just let me know
    when you've arrived.

Messages

Listen for them.

The messages that follow us from birth.

The ones demanding our full attention.

Life's first light carries us out of the watery shadows.

Introducing us – sometimes hesitantly,

    sometimes not –

        to tyranny's darkness and an ordinary death.

We soon enough detect an opening among the seekers.

Only to stumble and rise.

    And then stumble again.

With any luck,

    we may late find ourselves exchanging

        meaning for meaning

            and precision for gray.

Last steps, too, can reveal new beginnings.

Sometimes ones strewn only with gold-plated rubble

    and freshly painted facades.

But life's first light can carry us back to something more.

    Back to the beginning.

        Back to the watery shadows.

If we are among those still listening.

Remarkable

What's remarkable is the morning,
    with its disinfecting sunlight
        and fresh promises,
no matter where the night may have left you.

What's remarkable is the afternoon,
    with its opportunities to regroup
        and rethink
        and reorganize,
no matter how crazy the morning has been.

What's remarkable is the evening,
    with its quiet solitude
        and a chance to reflect,
no matter the successes or failures of the day.

What's remarkable is tomorrow.
    Every single day.

Thomas Zampino

Training and Pretending
(Healing After Surgery)

Working muscles from head to toe,

    slowly at first.

It's been a while,

    I need to build up my stamina.

Especially my mind

    which sometimes

        overwhelms with its flights

            into reality (reading the news.)

I step onto the platform

    with all of the others.

Pretending.

A Day in the Life

Candle flames flicker to the soft rhythm
    of the ceiling fan just above.
Digital cameras silently capture
    the very moment they are released.
Offering up evidence of time
    bookended by forward and backward realizations –
as if the present were nothing more
    than a highway rest stop
anchored between unmarked on-ramps and off-ramps,
    with a destination moving ever faster
even when we are standing still.

On Writing

Stringing together the exact right words,
   coffee and thesaurus in hand,
     somehow feels cold and calculated.
Like composing an argumentative legal brief.
Phrases too often sound stilted,
   without emotion –
     "just the facts ma'am"
in some rapid,
   machine gun like fashion
     or, heaven forbid,
       trite and obvious.
But I haven't yet figured a better way
   to approach the incredible gifts
     offered up right in front of me,
       just outside my kitchen window.

Apologies

Final words,

    trying to secure a lifetime of decision making

    that took unexpected turns through rough terrain.

I find myself no better off

    than if I had chosen to do everything differently

    or nothing at all.

Apologies are meaningless

    yet devastatingly imperative,

    a skill I learned about over the years

    but without much hard practice or reflection.

But this seems to be as good a time as any

    to sort things out.

Instructions for Dying

Who am I to question the timing
　　or even the plan itself?
Cells that first split without input or assent
　　are now consuming one another with abandon
　　　　in a race to the finish,
　　　　　　as if the survivor among them
　　　　　　　　will secure some form of immortality
　　　　　　or grand conclusion,
　　　　denying that they were long ago
　　programmed for self-disruption.
Details are still being followed to the letter,
　　only later instructing my brain
　　　　to neither challenge
　　　　　　nor cry
　　　　　　　　over circumstances
　　　　　　set in motion
　　　　a lifetime ago
　　– mostly
without input or dissent

synchronicity

Pristine Clarity

There's an outline of a tape
    that melted onto the dining room window,
    the one that faces our backyard.

It's in the shape of a small stop sign
    – eight sides
but with a little missing off the top
    – really only noticeable if you're looking for it.

I don't remember when it was first placed there
    but it likely held up some decoration
    for one of the kids' birthday parties.

Or possibly a celebrated drawing
    brought home from school,
    proudly displayed by the artist.

I suppose that a razor blade,
    a shot of window cleaner,
    and bit of elbow grease
    would make short order of it.

synchronicity

That I haven't done anything about it in all these years
  reminds me that I'm still awfully slow
  about exchanging childhood memories
  for a hint of pristine clarity.

Even if I can't seem to pinpoint
  the exact memory itself,
  only it's contours.

But then again,
  I'm in no particular hurry

                    to move on.

About the Author

Thomas Zampino lives in New York and has been an attorney for nearly 40 years. He began writing poetry only recently. His work has appeared in The University of Chicago's *Memoryhouse Magazine*, *Silver Birch Press*, *Bard's Annual 2019, 2020, 2021, and 2022*, *Trees in a Garden of Ashes*, *Otherwise Engaged*, *Chaos*, *A Poetry Vortex*, *Nassau County Voices in Verse*, *No Distance Between Us*, and *The Wonders of Winter*. His first book of poetry, *Precise Moment*, was published in 2021 and Brazilian director and actor Gui Agustini produced a video enactment of his poem *Precise Moment*.

He can be followed at:

https://thomaszampino.wordpress.com/

Previous Works by the Author

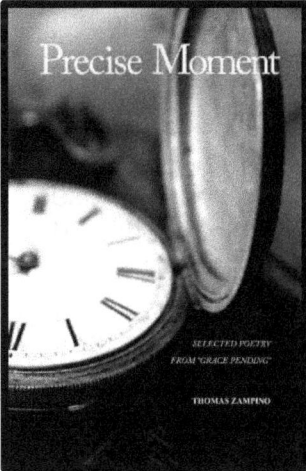

After nearly 40 years as a corporate and property tax attorney in New York City, Thomas Zampino's poems just about popped into existence at the ***Precise Moment*** when they could no longer be held back. This is a broad selection of mostly simple observations about life, faith, and meaning as seen through the eyes of someone who was profoundly touched by the world around him long before he realized it. Influenced by American poet Billy Collins and English poet David Whyte, these poems are a reflection of the aging - and hopefully the maturing - process in real time.

https://www.blurb.com/b/10812828-precise-moment-pb

Thomas Zampino

Acknowledgement

This book would not have been possible without the support, encouragement, and guidance of Southern Arizona Press (SAP) and its owner, Editor-in-Chief, and US Army veteran Paul Gilliland.

SAP is an incredible, mission-oriented publishing house whose sole purpose is to make the voices of "aspiring poets and authors available to a wide audience."

Paul, it has been my great honor to get to know you and I am profoundly grateful for this opportunity. Thank you!

www.ingramcontent.com/pod-product-compliance
Lightning Source LLC
Chambersburg PA
CBHW060806050426
42449CB00008B/1561